COMMUNITY • CONNECTIONS

?

WHAT'S IT LIKE TO LIVE HERE?
SUBURB

BY KATIE MARSICO

CHERRY LAKE
Publishing

Published in the United States of America by Cherry Lake Publishing
Ann Arbor, Michigan
www.cherrylakepublishing.com

Content Adviser: James Wolfinger, PhD, Associate Professor of History,
DePaul University, Chicago, Illinois
Reading Adviser: Marla Conn, ReadAbility, Inc.

Photo Credits: Cover and page 1, ©iStockphoto.com/jhorrocks; pages 5 and 21, ©Mat
Hayward/Shutterstock, Inc.; page 7, ©karamysh/Shutterstock, Inc.; page 9, ©Odua Im-
ages/Shutterstock, Inc.; page 11, ©Andreas Gradin/Shutterstock, Inc.; page 13, ©Inc/
Shutterstock, Inc.; page 15, ©bikeriderlondon/Shutterstock, Inc.; page 17, ©Zurijeta/
Shutterstock, Inc.; page 19, ©Thomas Barrat/Shutterstock, Inc.

LIBRARY OF CONGRESS CATALOGING-IN-PUBLICATION DATA
Marsico, Katie, 1980– What's It Like to Live Here?:
  Suburb / by Katie Marsico.
      pages cm. — (Community connections)
  Includes bibliographical references and index.
  ISBN 978-1-62431-568-8 (lib. bdg.) — ISBN 978-1-62431-592-3 (ebook) —
ISBN 978-1-62431-584-8 (pbk.) — ISBN 978-1-62431-576-3 (pdf)
  1. Suburbs — Juvenile literature. I. Title.
  HT351.M29 2014
  307.74—dc23   2013028550

Cherry Lake Publishing would like to acknowledge the
work of The Partnership for 21st Century Skills. Please
visit www.p21.org for more information.

Printed in the United States of America
Corporate Graphics Inc.
January 2014

SUBURB

CONTENTS

FROM BACKYARD TO BIG CITY

Tom and Kate played soccer in the backyard as their mom mowed the front lawn. Afterward, they rode their bikes to the park. Then the family drove to a nearby city. Together they visited a museum. Tom loved growing up in a suburb!

Kids in the suburbs often ride bikes to travel throughout their community.

LOOK!

Go online or head to your local library. Look up pictures of Milton, Ontario. This is a growing suburb of Toronto, Canada. Compare these photos to images of downtown Toronto. What differences do you notice? Do you see any ways the two places are the same?

A suburb is a **residential** area. A residential area is mostly homes, with few businesses. A suburb is located along the outer parts of a city. Suburbs usually have less **dense** populations or housing than cities. Most people in the suburbs live in single-family homes. Few suburban families live in apartments or other multifamily buildings.

Homes in the suburbs often have big yards.

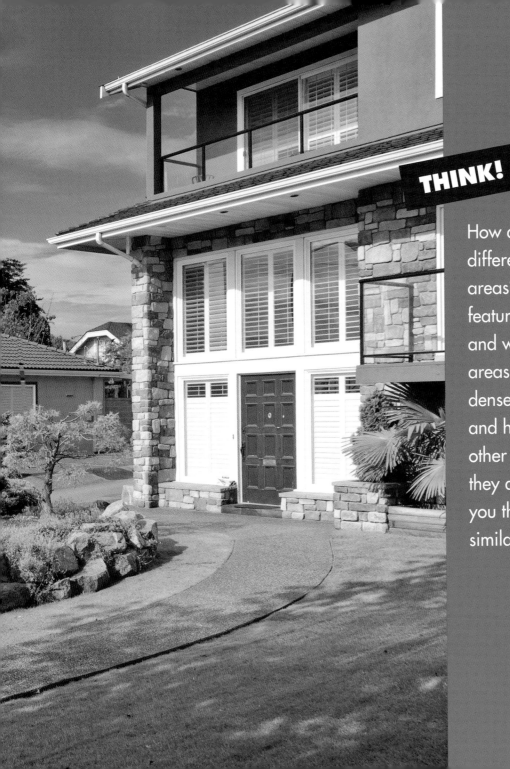

THINK!

How are suburbs different from **rural** areas? Suburbs feature less farmland and wilderness areas. They also have denser populations and housing. What other ways are they different? Can you think of any similarities?

7

Suburbs are good **communities** for growing families. Tom and Kate's family lived in a suburb to have plenty of space. They had a big yard to play in. Tom and Kate each had his or her own bedroom. Their parents worked in the city nearby. They **commuted** each day to get to their jobs.

Many people move to the suburbs when they want to start families.

Do you know adults who commute from suburbs to cities for work? Ask them how much time they spend traveling to work. How long does it take to travel home? Do they drive a car or take a bus or train?

DAY-TO-DAY LIFE

Tom and Kate took the bus to and from school. After school, Tom and Kate spent time with their friends. Tom also played hockey. Kate went to karate class. At home, they had chores. Kate took out the trash at night. Tom helped his mom with dishes after dinner.

Some suburbs have their own ice rinks where residents can play hockey.

Draw a picture of everyday life for a suburban child. Be sure to include the following details. What kind of house does he or she live in? Does the family own a car? Where does the child play with friends?

Some of their **responsibilities** are different from other kids' responsibilities. People in city apartments do not have their own backyard. Kids in the suburbs often do.

A backyard means extra space to play. It also means that there are extra outside chores. Kate helped her dad rake leaves. Tom helped pull weeds in the family's garden.

Autumn in some suburbs is a chance for kids to both rake and play in piles of colorful leaves.

THINK!

What pets do kids in the suburbs have? Many suburbs have rules against owning horses and other farm animals. Yet suburban residents often have different kinds of animals. These include fish, birds, cats, and dogs. With a big backyard, dogs have plenty of running space!

Cities have many kinds of public **transportation**. These include buses, trolleys, trains, and taxis. Transportation is different in the suburbs. Most suburban families use cars. Tom and Kate's family had two cars. Their parents gave them rides to their friends' houses. They also drove to stores, restaurants, and other businesses.

Most families in the suburbs own cars.

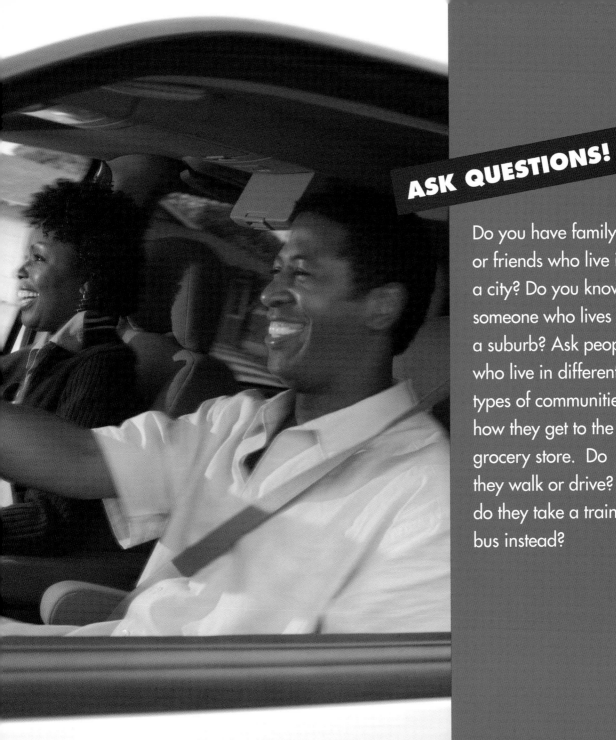

Do you have family or friends who live in a city? Do you know someone who lives in a suburb? Ask people who live in different types of communities how they get to the grocery store. Do they walk or drive? Or do they take a train or bus instead?

15

COMMUNITY FUN

There are many fun things to do in suburbs. Tom and Kate's favorite part of the summer was their neighborhood's block party. The neighbors talked, shared food, and played games. Tom and Kate also went to barbecues and ice cream socials.

Barbecues are a fun and tasty opportunity for neighbors to get to know each other.

MAKE A GUESS!

How do suburbs compare to cities in diversity? Can you guess? In the past, cities had far more diversity. A lot of suburbs had mainly white residents. Yet times are changing. Now suburban neighbors come from a wider variety of backgrounds.

17

THE BEST OF TWO WORLDS

Tom and Kate lived near a big city. This meant they had some of the excitement of city life. On weekends, their parents drove them to museums, theaters, or famous restaurants. Sometimes they took a train from their suburb to the city.

Trains make it easy to travel to and around a city.

Think about your top 10 favorite activities. Which could you do in a suburb? Are there any you could do only in a city? Do any need to be done in a rural area, such as a farm? Can you do some of these activities in all three places?

19

Tom and Kate enjoyed the best of two worlds. Big city life was close by. But back home, they still had parks and their backyard. This is why many people like living in the suburbs.

Parks are a great place for kids to play and make friends.

Build a model of a suburb. Make sure you include single-family homes. Backyards, shops, parks, and roadways are also important details. Do you have any material left over? Create a model of a nearby city, too!

21

GLOSSARY

communities (kuh-MYOO-nut-eez) places and the people who live in them

commuted (kuh-MYOOT-id) traveled some distance to work or school each day, usually by car, bus, or train

dense (DENS) crowded or thick

diversity (dye-VURS-uh-tee) variety

residential (rez-uh-DEN-chuhl) having to do with a neighborhood where people live

responsibilities (ri-span-suh-BIL-uh-teez) duties or jobs

rural (ROOR-uhl) having to do with the countryside or farming

transportation (trans-pur-TAY-shuhn) a way of moving people from one place to another

FIND OUT MORE

BOOKS

Bodden, Valerie. *A Suburb*. Mankato, MN: Creative Education, 2008.

Campbell, Stephanie. *The Little City Girl Meets the Suburbs*. Mustang, OK: Tate Publishing and Enterprises, 2011.

Flatt, Lizann. *Life in a Suburban City*. New York: Crabtree Publishing, 2010.

WEB SITES

BrainPOP Jr.—Rural, Suburban, and Urban
www.brainpopjr.com/socialstudies/communities /ruralsuburbanandurban/preview.weml
Learn more about life in different community settings, including suburbs, rural areas, and cities.

Houghton Mifflin Company—Types of Communities
www.eduplace.com/kids/socsci/books/applications/imaps/maps /g3_u1/
Use this interactive map to complete a variety of online activities connected to suburban, urban, and rural communities.

INDEX

ABOUT THE AUTHOR

Katie Marsico is the author of more than 100 children's books. She lives in a suburb of Chicago, Illinois, with her husband and children.